Path Through Wood    Sam Buchan-Watts

*for Ken Watts (1955–2021)*

# PATH THROUGH WOOD

All repetitions are intentional.

# Lines following

*'I have set you here'*

On the way into the woods, do you feel someone
turn the focus of the lens with the topmost parts
of their forefinger and thumb –
in line with the crick of your neck, as you turn to look
but feel the head fixed straight. The branches tick,
someone set them going. The woods have set you here,
so as to feel away from thoughts, but still you think
*I never really entered.* The way into the woods is in a way
to go round the woods: the woods are always in the way
when you're in them (if they're woods). The way in
weighs on the memory of summer like a cloak hung
over the sun. The way in is an act of hyphenation,
a statement about the weather, the weather in the woods.

ballad

glare does its fluorescent spider, greenery fidgets, what twitches, waking after a long sleep    lines knot in protest at 'I'    beneath the lithe long grass that swallows the path    ballad, ballade, roach, a vintage alloy    heard a cough indicating copse or corpse    hoped to swap quarrel with communion drenched bracken    leonids, lighters crammed with dirt, murky translucence, cigarette cherry a jewel of heat, a signet ring, a sovereign state    laminated signage, condensation, water retention on the lung    the wood's en-dash    the closure of wood    the woodland sings, the woodland stinks deodorant sting    chill afterburn    the seal of its fridge withered, weak    roots feel for closure or release    find rusted pulleys, quaint dusty canopy in need of husbandry    corrupted membrane reconfigures green    empty promise of springe    beyond that screen    bare board    ballad    has been

'pleasant sutherings of the shade' fine    for childhood's 'elaborate inner space'    bleached plastic    hands making steeple    lonely cathedral    to burr or to burrow  unlawful burial    to be spun out    to white out    from the crowd    forest floor    a stage    the woods' bookcase its muttering inhibitions    dirty magazines    gateway drugs    dirt is shit    at what gradation    boys brittle in the woods        epochal summer    where you bury the past    the path not taken

what could we hide here    hope it's grown over    jim carey energy    abattoir slurry    the children's book    laughing gas canister    whatever predecessor        moral tincture    lean    learned        enlightened  left where it was found

'The Days Go Just Like That'

If you emerge from the glove of woods –
the trail's patchiness like jaundiced spliff paper
and the dry powder bloom of a fire extinguisher
let off by kids last night –
blinking, feeling skew-whiff, confused, to find this:
a medieval reenactment *in medias res*
then you have seen it exactly as it should be seen,
exposed, but distant, so that the quirks –
the radiant tinkle, the gather of enthusiasts,
the rhubarb-rhubarbs, the unintelligible frills,
the coarseness of sound their makeshift dress makes
like brown paper crumpling as it's being burnt –
are so correct, as if history were a thing to be administered
in the afternoon. And the hold-all blue
seems about to decompress, until all we have left
is a far-off clobber of wood. And the days go just like that.

## Coastal Scene

to pollute or purify the air
or the air's fringes
what's the difference
down here
in the ditches
and the skatepark put
naturally with the cesspit

## Pillar of Smoke

beyond there is a hut smoked out by
paintball the man loved the game
because of very few rules the chance
he might be mistaken as benign in his mask

men play at boys playing men
the chemical smoke tinged by artificial
colourings like cake mix pushed,
without pain, to the back of the phrase

behind black smoke is guy ropes
like hurt behind the fingernail
pressed to see if it is dirt or bruising
the flattened veneer of canvas

# Tableaux

## *Coulisse*

He acts as if deception is the plainest thing,
while a flat piece of scenery hides at the edge

of the stage or in its wings, or the science-
lab-cum-dressing room or the space between

the buildings and the mobile classrooms, the birds
and the birds' wings, or the mirror with its brownish

mix of poster-painted primary colour confused
with a dirty window or screen, or slab of water

ready to slide from off- to centre-stage,
and the narrow frame not in line with its rollers

squealing with what you are about to see
or that which you have already seen.

*Cornice*

Or that which you have already seen, and not retained.
The safety curtain never lifted. The curtain painted.

That season our feelings were fixed in the room's corners,
out of view but not invisible. Ornate not ostentatious.

The white cube gallery was invented in response, he said,
to what was seen as a crisis of cornice, throwing us.

We needed theatre's frayed edge to be on the surface,
baroque, felicitous. His voice sounded fulsome yet cold

and in that moment it was the length of the room.
I was lost and missed the quaint corners joining decor

and form and that which we cannot hear or hold in view
or square with the venetian blinds we struggle to see through.

*Conus*

Or square with the venetian blinds we struggle to see through,
the market square, the blackboard's flimsy border, repressed boy's

faded capriccio stuck badly to the bedroom wall. The teacher
had been saying that just because the world depicted precedes

the film it's no less made, the rear-view traffic no less art.
The frame tempers chance: what is made in the finding

is found in design. His delivery was well practised, but I found him
hard to parse among the poem's phrasing, the ventricles of its heart,

low extremity of the spinal cord. In the operating theatre
is the intricacy of parts any more on view? Collateral rarely offers

a dress rehearsal, this much is true. The frame might be found,
discarded or applied, the onus is nonetheless on you.

## Onus

Discarded or applied, the onus is nonetheless on you,
he said, since once an image is seen and lodged

in the mind it can't easily be unseen. I didn't know
what relation this had to the unconscious or the unquiet,

yet didn't think it worth asking. Then he swerved
and said what happens offscreen is the scariest bit.

I found a lot of this hard to accept. I had some idea
how bad things could get. I began to feel the hang

of his words like a costume that can't unsee the film,
forgets the text, its desire to touch every part of the body

like cold water, wading out into a soliloquy I could not
have foreseen. I lost him there beyond that screen.

*Prompt*

The poem's form a set of shapes in worn-white tape on stage frayed
slightly at the edges in a way that would be difficult to recreate
by hand, or peel off and reapply to another stage, though as they say
anything's possible when the house lights go down. It conflates

the set of shapes and the crime they demarcate if the crime is
a part of the stage, the theatre, the building's façade, long since faded.
The poem's form a set of shapes in worn-white tape, frayed by the arid
heat of lights which obfuscates these lines, provides no shade.

*HAMLET: Nor did you nothing hear?*
*GERTRUDE: No, nothing but ourselves.*

Listening In
(Fresh Claim for Asylum)


He is telling me again about the head and the heart,
that the head won't think without the heart which beats,
and the heart that beats for god, or because god gave it to us
or because god lives in us. Can you create a plant like that?
No. So god exists. Much of our allotted time is taken up with this.
Or that the head is a satellite broadcasting out, while
the ears receive; they're small, by comparison, with less potential.
I half-listen, trying to think of the poem by George Herbert
which is about the majesty of god's creation, and not
the plant pot's harsh plastic clutching after terracotta,
the lucid green of his coffee cup, the dehydrated box of tissues.
At the urinal, I listen to him shit. Sound contained poorly
within the stall. It shakes, unembarrassed, articulate. The outside
blue we enter differently is a blank slate, incorrigibly deep.

Happy Accidence

'What does your wordless absence say'
if I speak language then language
confides against its better nature – I
hear it rounding closer in on quiet

the mind's ear leans in in awkwardness
at rest only at its own crests,
pushing penny coins off the steel
shelf without much premeditation or will

your rhyme there for the foot to find
a stirrup – nonsense catches, clots
then folds together in cheery pleats,
a mound of fabric compact for being neat

Sounds Inside

*a private moment splintered with observation*

I am overhearing a documentary on Radio 4 about music cultures in UK prisons, listening to the
friend I am currently living with, a medical professional at the local prison, listen

as he tries to manage the weekend kitchen, clearing up after his boisterous child, the clamour of
clutter re-joining the kitchen's ambience, his son

has opted not to harass him while I am in the living room, one of two living rooms I might choose
from, where I amble about in order to linger

longer than I would if I was in there with him, talking idly so as to avoid his son's chaotic attention,
and discover that my friend likes the programme more than I anticipate, given

what he's seen and heard, how left-to-die the industry is in the broader hierarchy of attention, and
notice that my friend's rhythm in the house as the owner – though I want to qualify this

with the conditions unique to him: part-owner, late in life, no help, etcetera – is different from mine
as lodger, and the over-identification with the family I feel

in my satellite proximity, a position that feels precarious though well intentioned, demonstrable love
offset with what's pragmatic – a balance we all, by degrees, manage, though my friend

is invested more than most in alternative kinship in a lived way, indeed, has been more present
this year than any member of my family, and – since this isn't about me – he truly believes

that medical aid be provided indiscriminately, a fact not distinct from why he's dedicated so much
time to working in prisons, why he has begun to see so much life

in terms of structure, during the irregular time off he gets for childcare – the rhythm of the
supermarket on weekday afternoons, the gym in which toddlers trampoline

supervised behind nets for fifteen-minute periods, with its smell of socks, I suppose, the baptist
church perched awkwardly on a double roundabout, its Monday playgroup

costing a few pounds, his mortgage, with its morbid scaling and punitive fees, paid for by his work
at the prison, this all being, broadly speaking, a means of organising experience,

which would be a convenient basis for a poem, the space articulated between my listening and his,
the interaction of domesticity and kinship, a diagram

of listening, the threshold between inner and outer ear, levels of sound and significance, but all of this might complicate the simple fact I am listening

more to my friend, whose working life is unique among the people I know, than to the documentary and the reflections he makes afterwards because, though he does his best

not to bring the prison home with him, I have felt it hardening his world, even if I hesitate to say it hardens him, a world where inmates frequently attack the healthcare staff, whose ear

is the only ear available in an environment in which my friend is forbidden to walk more than ten steps with a set of keys in hand, where a door must be closed newly each time

it is walked through, a disingenuous response to corrupting violence, a man smokes spice through a ventolin inhaler but sleeps with it lit, waking with a polyester football

shirt burned to his body, a proximity of atrocity I find profound, take special pride in telling people about my friend, hearing their attention lift, feeling the contour

of their ear, their voice going sombre, hop the fence between responsible inquiry and a rawer curiosity, meanwhile

two men in a prison in South London are so fearful of leaving their shared cell they listen to the radio all day, which is transportive, without the inclination to read in it

a poem, in a built environment in which there are no lie-ins, where the ear is, as Lacan says, the only orifice that cannot be closed, though I am not convinced Lacan considered the status

of the orifice in prison, where you might use a phone supplied by Samaritans, but it has to be requested and delivered and men have to be resourceful, boil baked

beans in a kettle, one inmate in London crushes biscuit and hoovers it up in a multifaith chapel just to hear the difference in sound, to carve out space in which he might hear

what, I don't know, textural difference, transformation, something that necessarily I cannot get near, though I can go in and see my friend, forgo our habitual speech acts and hold him

to me, awkwardly, yet choose to make do with the sound of his pottering, that he is brewing a second pot of coffee this late in the morning

(for Matthias Connor)

## Gigha

the ear instructs the eye to wade out with sound,
long legs without waders give thanks
listening to sounds lost to the mingling of water

which makes them. Rhymes etched on the waves
each time they subside, 'unique & miraculous',
the water strides out from its shores in great hoops.

## Listening In

It's apt I'm teased for speaking one language
by a group of refugees who've been displaced
for most of their lives, these boys are puckish
with disbelief, deliberately withholding, I suspect,
their English, or am I paranoid: a fear of
boys in groups, of conspiration, a ball kicked
from nowhere to the back of the head, presides
as I prepare to help teach them about the public
phone box: what it means to make a call
with this antique tech hiding in plain sight,
for a group whose smartphones are a lifeline –
the phone call a useful metaphor
for poetry's one-sided intimacy, the art
an instrument for academic public engagement –
as I invite the boys in turn to leave a message
on my colleague's answerphone while
their peer group jeers through a door frame
long since retired of glass, exposing them,
rescinding the object's inherent discretion,
the message may be for anyone, I say: living, dead
or otherwise, nobody is listening on the end
of the line, not this time, and that is good,
speak without fear of being misunderstood,
but the boys look more perplexed about where
the money goes than the message or the medium,
who can blame them, so I retain my research
on the booth as embodiment of our interior,
of privacy and confession, national kitsch,
more honest would be to point to universals:

vandalism, caustic stink of piss, I could quote
to them Marshall McLuhan: the booth over-
turns an abstract 'regime of "time" and "space"',
if I did not cringe at the use of 'regime' in this sense,
if I did not fear an inclination to rephrase experience,
to get anxious about how I looked or how
this sounds, how even here I skirt the question
of speaking 'for' in staking common ground.

# Borderline Decisions

the subject will have a well-founded fear
but not so as to flee their dispersal area
volunteers trade classes on elocution
for training in refugee action over coffee                *I don't follow it up*

hypertension developed due to threats
founded, establish or originate in belief
the judges serving in Lahore, dense and difficult
replied that he had lied to save his life                 *I wrote 'have' in my notes*
                                                          *at Bradford Tribunal*

which even in recall renews the fear,
in well-weighed syllables, WhatsApp messages
family reunion, may exhaust the credible
if found detained, well founded as well persecuted

## Listening In

'You won't go listening in, will you, to our conversation on the landing,' though they could have had it in the kitchen. The bedroom was set down two steps below the landing, a window placed high looking down into it: ideal for listening in and not being seen. Being spied upon. Listening in with military efficiency, or military effectiveness, whichever is the least defective. The squaddies are shown gory videos depicting the reality of war, he told her. Maybe then, maybe earlier. She told me, some time before, there's nothing worse than a man screaming in pain, you can't suppress it. A questionable proposition, or position, whichever is the least affective. She will never hear from him again. I never heard the conversation to begin with.

'We don't just hear you, we listen'


You do not have to qualify to get someone to listen,
but it helps to keep them interested, since a cry born
of desperation may burst like a fountain's first ejaculation
of water up past etiquette but still lands predictably
in its concrete basin. The question 'so what do you think
your next step should be?' casts the steep drop down
to the next unknowable. Its well-meant firmness
a stone weighing down the throat. Hard to evade
without hiding under the slats again or their equivalent.
And yet this listening phoneline sags
unobtrusively like a retired bungee cord,
cradling the ear we share as it says,
'try and remember, there is no right answer'.

# Cloud Study

*The observations*
*about self-consciousness*
*As one subclass*
*of those determinations*
*Every squiggle serves*
*the composition*
*A vase containing*
*water, or even*
*a cloud*

Cloud Study
Cloud Study (after Cozens's *Engravings of Skies*)


Cloud-benighted, deathly stillness
The clouds preceded us

Streaky cloud at the top of the sky
Intermixture of the sky and the landscape


Cloudless at first
Clouds pass and disperse

Study of Clouds
Study of Clouds


In a sky full of clouds, clouds upon clouds
Everything but the clouds

Cloud Study
Study of Clouds


Stratus      Cumulus
Cirrus       Cloudland

Sky above Clouds IV
Study of a cloudy sky
Study of Cumulus Clouds
Coastal Scene with Cliffs


Calibri over Times New Roman
page break
over two columns
Chiaroscuro

In the Realms of the Unreal
Clouds to be drawn
tailed by roiling monster clouds


Let the stormy clouds chase

Sunset at sea after a storm
Seascape Study with Rain Cloud
Seascape with Rain Cloud
Snow Cloud
Rain


when the horizon fades
awful rainbow

*going to pieces*
        *falling for ever*

            *loss of sense of real*

                ~ DW WINNICOTT

# You just know

that boundaries exist to be tested, and everyone knows
(because he won't shut up about it) that the boy on the back
row of the coach coming home from Ypres needs to masturbate
and is going to have to wait at least four and a half hours to *tame
the snake*, and the only way to get in the flat-headed straws of
sherbet is to bite them, which is of course crude, as crude as having
a password for the sweet deal for those coming back from Ypres.
And the road to Calais seems to bend indefinitely, and the coach
chucks itself and the weight of these lives held at great speed
between the oncoming reams of coaches on their way
to Ypres and the rows of sugary trees pristine in their little collars
of cable tie. And someone managed to get stoned, to bring with
him the coppery smell, and it's there in the corrosive tangerine
of the tractor coughing smoke, ploughing fields of salted caramel and
which might veer off beyond them, threshing mounds of concrete,
chewing up rats and benign snakes in the grass before plunging
into bunkers and ditches, and further, the networks of pipes,
before emerging with an uneven bounce, heroically unseen,
on the brow of a hill with a wistful bump to say it's rare
for a thing to stay immaculate, except the glassy light of Ypres.

## A Mess

I had to nip my tongue.
I was so young.

I asked him questions
questions I thought he liked

about what can kill a man
so many his answer

overheats in anger
like a livewire

the source of fire is unclear.
Even a BB gun can kill you

if it gets you point blank
behind the roof of your mouth.

I thought it might get him to like me
when he wasn't mock drowning me.

Instead I made a mess of my youth
stood by the bath mesmerised

by this angry man's penis
slumped like a drunk

in the couch of its scrotum
the warm patch barely

beneath the water a crude
softness unnervingly in reach.

Asking question after question
this is how I touched him

scratched his scorching
parts with brittle arms

so I learnt to tongue the soft membrane
behind the roof of my mouth

to strain its root
out of its habit.

## Colouring In

*'That's the way we were made. We can't help it.'*
John Ashbery, *Girls on the Run*

Chicago is the home of INTUIT on Milwaukee Avenue, *The Center for Intuitive and Outsider Art*. 'Outsider' is a contested category but mostly means art produced beyond academies, categories, canons: cultural production offset with its medium, works made with naïve materials, street waste, Prell bottles, drawing in crayon and coloured pencil.

An academic symposium, a two-day discussion, ends with a private view of the permanent collection of Henry Darger for delegates and dinner. Nearby the museum is a railway carriage repurposed as a retro diner. In the museum yellowing kitsch is furnished with an unearthly status, across the street it's upcycled by the robust economy of service.

Within INTUIT and the petrified scent of the A/C, Darger's little Vivian Girls flee and/or give chase across panoramas, the pale floral battlefield vistas he imagined hung like precious scrolls. Each moment in the scenes assumes equal prominence, each proliferating reversal. The flatness of his girl gangs and Glandelinian men, their familiar outlines cut from comics, belies the mutilation and more beguiling ambiguities, the way they cluster like cultures of bacteria. Watery mirror made thin with child's paint. Images barely seen, prime for burning, the kind you can't leave at the scene, when playtime's over and it's time for tea.

John Ashbery shared Darger's boyhood vocabulary, Little Annie Rooney, Buster Brown, he opts – to different ends – to reinscribe a legacy from those materials: blood-red suit, stoned eyes, colluding dogs. Henry impaled his girls, rolled them up in floor rugs like pigs in blankets. From Henry's wars John drew rhubarb stains on Peggy's frock that match its rickrack trim. Textiles both lovingly stitched and shoehorned in.

Beyond the exhibition is a partitioned area, a room within a room, Henry Darger's apartment-cum-studio reconstructed, from which he has always left for mass or work, represented by the art materials he collected, the outline of an interior for us to colour in:

> elastic bands soiled by dirty hands,
> shoes, buttons, eyeglasses, balls of string
> aged with the homework trick of a dip
> in tea, but here it's darker, filter coffee,
> the blemish of moral tinctures – primary
> colours, clouds, childhood, blood –
> the hoard of craft materials, the pulpy
> catholic imagery, magazines tied devotionally
> in stacks, comic strips, ads and other means
> of colonising the child's attention,
> to keep it fixed in two dimensions,
> definite lines, the nascent anger of the 'I'.

The smear of anxious threat beneath the jubilance of Edward Lear, the skewed perspective of the Lilliput, laid bare.

The gentle Darger Scholar greets each delegate in turn with the collector's unwavering keenness, his fingers delicate in misty latex gloves.

Here are systems of organisation to please the most boyish: his love of the compact, sequestered places, sugary treats, hardened cake pigment in strips, annotated tracing, knick-knacks, bric-à-brac. Joseph Cornell was to find home amidst the little of his gleanings from

Flushing's dimestores and his brother's train sets, to make nests in boxes for his desires, dead insects and other keepsakes. The intimacy of an imagined homemade machine. There is the presiding feeling that somewhere an underground tunnel leads to a secret hatch in a tree.

Like kids, we prefer to handle objects in their pliant, most suggestive state. To find in Cornell's studio the glasses, balls, birds, plastic shells, and corking, over conscription and asylum for feeble-minded children after excessive masturbation. The unseen illustrations left by the dead artist. Colouring books not yet marked by *64 different brilliant colors in Crayola.*

'Crayon' derives from *craie*, the French for chalk. In *Modern Painters* Ruskin refers to chalk debris, black and white, broken off the crayons Turner used. Ruskin drew Rose La Touche, his little white statue in the woods,

> who by shading
> rose made pale
> and elegant frottage
> sought to diminish

As a man who lived with and through art, he seemed unable to disentangle Rose from his aesthetic theories, even as she haunted his dreams, says the critic, as if that's the way he was made.

Crayon does not shade. It has the jumbo quality of childhood as we would like most children to imagine it: chunky lines of uncomplicated colour, immutable but machine washable, firm as a well-kept bedtime. Darger offsets unhygienic brown with anaemic baby blue. Eyes and mouths plunging deep beyond the dimensions of their frame, as a bullet might be said to.

A child is rarely alone, though he may be let loose, each space for play highly predetermined so as to not fall out of the world, to pop down a large rabbit hole under a hedge.

To stand in a kitchen observing a child draw with such focus as to be alone in the world is to watch him draw himself out of the world. Is to become, in that moment, that child, to overturn the world, like Henry Darger in Chicago with his Vivian Girls.

The younger the child the more likely he is to draw over the lines printed for colouring within. The bird may exceed the confines of its wooden box, the dream interpretation the content of the dream, when the stricture of colouring in becomes discipline. Some colour as if that's the way they were made, they can't help it, others so not to take up space. Some to confront, or because to confront what's beyond colouring is paralysing.

From crayon to pen is graduation: pen's firmer, less redeemable. It's a holding space, a tool that may be inscribed with discipline. And yet the child peeks out in parapraxes, slips of the tongue. He doesn't care for the canon. Children like repetition, flirt only to find its limit.

§

Vladimir Nabokov took pleasure situating his transgressions in discipline – though the relative benefits of that have proven to be a matter of opinion. He sought out grammatical slips and subjugation. He taught us to make ornaments of accidents, that for 'fountain' read 'mountain', for 'comic', 'cosmic'.

His ridiculous villain Charles Kinbote has the collector's eccentricity. He collected his love, the bad gray poet John Shade, and may – in loving – eclipse him, or become him, sublimating desire into *Pale Fire*'s baroque creation.

Kinbote installed two ping-pong tables for twins and another boy, another boy, which function in the novel to foreground his unrepentant homosexuality and to distinguish 'game' from 'play'. Perhaps it's fair to say that games have rules to stick to, 'play' more keenly evokes a boundary which may be defined, pushed, subtly transgressed without crossing. C. L. Dodgson's boat rides with Alice Liddell kept, of course, within the Thames or Isis, licked by water heard and not seen, between bounds of the riverbanks, lolloping clouds, Christchurch Quad, Chartreuse for the Senior Common Room.

Nabokov translated Carroll into Russian, exalting him, as Ashbery does the paper Darger glued with water paste to make large pieces, puts crayon and colouring into the canon. Invoking the serious matter of play, to act as though – as Humpty Dumpty does – for three hundred and sixty-four days of the year it's your 'un-birthday'.

'The rhyme is the line's birthday', claims Nabokov's speaker on Russian Poetry – joining a host of critics who assign to rhyme a life, gender, agency. Carol Mavor boldly claims that 'critics try to veil the obvious sexuality that Carroll captured on photographic plates', offering rhyme a possible corollary.

The speaker declares: 'there are certain customary twins / in Russian as in other tongues [...] but sun / and wind and life and death [rhyme] with none',

> Nabokov is arch in his decision
> to not distinguish the pronoun
> 'none' from the implied 'no rhyme',
> nothing, a ghost of 'nonsense',
> rendered by the poem's cadence.

Darger casts the skies in storm cloud purple, the texture of a bruise, but afternoons in July, if fair and cloudless, are apt to be narcotic, with the blue above and the watery mirror below.

The INTUIT gallery is silent but for the squeak of feet on polished concrete, the well-meaning self-regard of the scholars' gazing.

From form's precipice difficulty hangs: without the elegant bounds of chess, nonsensical refrain, magazines tied in stacks, the lines for colouring in, this ground is precarious.

There is always somewhere a child too bound to the play area to stop and say that was that for the day; it may be Darger, it will be another, drawn to crayon and pencil, too fearful to stop colouring, unconscious as he does of the paper's darkening, of the weight his blunt implement is pressing. He might scratch out a realm behind the paper, get stranded there.

Sky Pavilion

We trust the power lines to run forever overhead
       to cover our intimacies
and itineraries: taxes and car stereos

      schools that double as evacuation halls
a man who will dutifully come
      to fix the wires when we don't see him
there is always one like him to call

Just before the envelope is torn
               in a village some miles down
a boy is testing his voice on the comfy
      confine of his childhood bedroom
letting himself fester for the first time

He spins a globe by the acid light of his computer
         in dim winter, stabs an accusatory finger
at random; tears a hole in its fabric as the power cuts out

## Dew Point

Bored with no thought the boy draws with his finger a
dick on layers of ancient dicks he does not yet connect
drawing with desire. Curses new in the mouth condense
the atmosphere of the school bus randy with
adolescence. He doesn't make a link between the
medium of drawing breath and the spit the window's
syrupy residue leaves. Early actions as stone
inscriptions when mark-making and thinking are the
same. Inside the bus a lobbed pepsi bottle the fester of
the end of the end of the day kept to swill around inside
some loose tooth blood and drained pimple. The
chemical action the process develops is undevelopable.
The weak last breath in the lynx can is talking
underwater. The subject-matter of which constitutes
thinking mutual relations come later. Half asleep this
morning the pissing boy sees germs squirm op-art
crushing cloudy in the toilet bowl. The day before's
cortisol the body not yet learnt to keep hold. The
impression Freud drew dicks before interpretation
came. Germy drops of condensation on the reinforced
glass when he used *verdichten* for the dream work inheres
compressed inside the word itself. At some point a form
catches in the writer's mind when the dew point is raised
to an ambient temperature. One can convince oneself in
all such cases to wake up but never grasp its suspended
apparent unendingness. A consciousness spoiled like
food full of its own and others' desires added too quickly
to the fridge while never having proof the condensation

draws attention to itself. Each drop round in itself encloses a rune. The loneliness of the earnest boy a man who can't not help himself to the leftovers saved for lunch tomorrow. The steamy bus absorbs the coughing fabric full of vapour. The process of reduction is coming into logical relations from without. A watched pot incomplete towards evening. Somewhere becoming rain written in dew is the window of the dream.

Pavilion Complex

*'My characters are… outside my inner self
like the mournful monsters of a cathedral façade'*
  Vladimir Nabokov

As a boy he dreamed a pavilion twice a year
independently of the dream's subject-matter
just as it was, if not more perfect – a version
of a pavilion out in summer nineteen fourteen.

Independently of dreams' subject-matter
is the dark vista of their imagining, how things appear.
Of a pavilion out in summer nineteen fourteen
he chose to dream, night and day…

Is the dark vista of their imagining how things appear
to the stained-glass artist Nabokov created?
He chose to dream, night and day,
he was a cathedral, his own grandiloquent pavilion!

## Pigeon Grey

I dreamt the pigeons were stressful to look at because of their own stress, which is deep down where their guts are like the place the tube goes in the afterhours. Pigeons grey at their core like seaside rock, black toenails emerging from their blunt feet. It was a moot point of history when a pigeon was forced to wash its coat only in the great grey fountain; grey like speed sweating and hot in its national lottery stub, a discrete kind of carrier. I dreamt that pigeons long for a vestibule marked off from the sky, something to slip into, to have the remaining sky fold over the gap, and that pigeons appear afflicted because affliction is the only means of engagement with a sky they hate deep down in their toenails, toenails clacking lightly on the unkind floor. Where to hide from a sky, how to fall out of it? Their feet stick on the ground in collaboration – stick to its Maltesers and other treats we leave and still we hate them for this. They walk awkwardly in the way a person would fall. They think about affliction and the euphemism of the word 'fall' for those who fall in battle on any grey Tuesday in regular midwinter, and they pity them

## The art of trying

I always told the truth and told it slant, often at right angles, crossed like a constructivist movement, or lines on a cutting mat, and my speech was deliberate, each word a part in a speech act I had forethought, that was all mine and not corrupted by the day and its crowding condensations, its creeping willow and moss. Through the leaves came a light, hot with acid-like ambition, running past the branches of whatever was outside. I saw my language like a history of brief romances – threadbare, synoptic, a relic of automation.

The 'I' speaks out and disperses; one line drawn, walked, criss-crossed on the cutting mat unseen beneath the poem. I told the truth with a grand design including spirals, folded pleats, matchstick lighthouses, all interlacing; nothing was straightforward when put together, or even implicitly so, and therefore none of this can be recorded, legibly written down, redacted, laid to rest in a pitch black drawer, held back, held against me, held down in shallow water.

Forum Bar

To leave a digital footprint that's out of step
with Stradishall, Suffolk. Some future
for the son of a former
British Baptist Minister.
To smile wide in the face of
grey rain / atopic eczema
– smile not wiped by
computer / tabloid paper. To have
considered all the evidence and data,
to rock the boat so as to touch both
sides of the water – people died for the right
to see the evidence, others kept on constant watch
/ psychotropic medication so as to hold
some semblance of the smiling / guilty person.

(for Lauri Love)

## Computer Fraud and Abuse Act

To give back borrowed data
no meaningful return of what's stolen
when everyone gets a copy
'return' as submit, split from 'recall'
retract, undo send / these shadows offended
behind a bike helmet / ACER laptop
to access material produced at public research
institutions / private institutions with public funding
via public WIFI / in a network closet at MIT
the online equivalent of checking
too many books out of the library
people are still talking confidently
in terms of online equivalents
the integrity of the printed object
he could be lending them out
could be boyish curiosity / a fine line
between merely imp / and prison camp
buying or borrowing a culture with a poster
for a meticulous planner / bankrupting
everyone you know / barristers' chambers
of the heart / breaking and entering
beautiful smiling boy / is it not about
everything you put out into the world
no return / no valency / sorry

(for Aaron Swartz)

*the nameless other boys*
*are clambering too*
*through floorboards*
*and tree trunks*
*to a compartment*
*in the sea*
*in a tree*
*in the house*
*in the mind*


*on the visual plane*
*of the artist's work*
*which in regression*
*submerges him*
*and from which he later*
*wakes with a scream*

## Cloud Study

condensation after the internet
loop lines and short circuits
the presence on instant messenger
both permanent and always too abrupt
mutual relations come later
its thin goat-paths of association
the density of the air is no metaphor
clouds roll on like metre
unconscious surface of the water
the juice with its weak constitution
a plastic picture of the process
see how the orient dew

The Subject of Landscape
The landscape is still life


One day clouds muffin against a tinny sky
And he led them in a cloud by day

Ruskin sulks the way to Chamonix
        plodding stroppy cloud
                Schuyler's neediness
                        his 'washed dust clouds'
                                caught in a logbook
Proust's buried curls in the pillow
        goose down cloud
                smothers the ear canal
                        Barthes plays prisoner's base
                                the feeling not of corralling but freeing
                                not bounds, un-
                                    bounding others

child makes us climb inside a cloud
I'd cloud your common sense

clouds to be drawn
Clouds of Gold

backlit because they are
took Constable an hr

Clouds of Witness
iambic filler
Storm cloud purple
Tincture of the skies

## The Days Just Go Like That

Once you re-submerge tipsy and lightly bereft,
cursing your way backwards
into a haze that's styled by trees, you may feel
like an arm retreating into an unwelcoming sleeve,
and realise that the woods cannot smother without an opening
or the roaming shadow of the sun, stopping at the pathway.
You try to hold the re-enacted scene in your mind
but now you are out of it, the dream of medieval jousting
is just smattering, and the turf track is quickening,
along with the remnants of hash resin
and benzedrine, and filaments of rubber, and the way it all slides
muted across the colour cones of your eyes
and the clomping of your feet is almost separate
and singular, as the insides of a fire extinguisher –
emptied of its starch and fibre – still retain a fundamental structure,
and there's a city down here somewhere.

## Plinth

some things are hard to not do fully
going to vote

as opposed to voting on
giving way for another driver

giving thanks in return
what about to listen or to look back

at a plinth in the Louvre
to break the syntax

to 'do' the Louvre, to not expect
form to reflect back glitteringly

which is surely the sea's difficult
sleight of hand and
the sea only

(for Edward Doegar)

## The Word Pavilion

We woke feeling most baffled
by the removal of things: what is
left out for a damp autumn to rot?
The pavilion is thin and unable to fend
for itself. The suburb hasn't room
for its shabby opulence, delicate
as a wasp dried on the sill.

The boy runs out into the garden and marks
in chalk a rhomboid where he imagines
the pavilion might have been. What use in
the remark 'autumn is coming', when the roof
isn't there to catch it? The word 'pavilion'
dismantles when he goes to use it
like an old washing peg. The phrase 'a chance of rain'
might go in its place; but the weather changes.

NOTES

There are many voices consciously and unconsciously invoked but not explicitly cited in the work. This list includes, but is not limited to, Frances Leviston, Edmund White, Michael Moon, Sandra Simonds, Roger Gilbert, Walter de la Mare, Robert Sheppard.

*Pillar of Smoke* (1964) is a painting by Karl Weschke.

'Happy Accidence' and 'Gigha' are written towards the work of Denise Riley.

'Sounds Inside' is named after a podcast made for Prison Radio by Carl Cattermole.

'Borderline Decisions' quotes from the definition of 'refugee' in the Geneva Refugee Convention and Protocol.

'We don't just hear you, we listen' is a distinction made by both Roland Barthes and Samaritans.

*Cloud Study* is an expanded cento.

'Pigeon Grey' was commissioned as a response to the artwork *Bristow* (2016) by Adel Abdessemed.

'Forum Bar' was a change in legislation whereby British courts 'may bar prosecution overseas if it is in the interests of justice to do so'. Lauri Love is a British activist charged with cyber-attacks against the US government between October 2012 and October 2013.

Aaron Swartz was an American computer programmer and activist prosecuted in 2011 for violating the Computer Fraud and Abuse Act after downloading academic articles from the not-for-profit JSTOR that were freely available via MIT; he killed himself in January 2013. The poem quotes David Segal of Demand Progress.

## ACKNOWLEDGEMENTS

Thank you to the editors of the following publications where these poems first appeared: *Bristow* (Bold Tendencies); *The Caught Habits of Language: An Entertainment for W. S. Graham for Him Having Reached One Hundred*; *Fieldnotes Journal*; *Hotel*; *In the Round – Renewal* (Kelder Projects); *likestarlings*; *The London Magazine*; *Poetry London*; *The Poetry Review*; PROTOTYPE; *The Rialto*; *The White Review*; *The World Speaking Back…To Denise Riley*.

Part of *Cloud Study* was published as a chapbook by If a Glyph Falls in 2020.

Sincere thanks to the following for your help with this book: Tom Rees, Kit Buchan, Sam Riviere, Matt Welton, Olly Todd, Caleb Klaces, Lucy Mercer, Matthew Holman, Linda Kemp, J. T. Welsch and Hugh Haughton; to Wolfboy and Rachal Bradley, Sandy and Kaspar; to Matthew Stuart, Andrew Walsh-Lister and my extraordinary publisher, Jess Chandler; to Edward Doegar, my best, most holding ear; and to Rebecca Birrell, my love, who taught this book to be boyish.

I'm grateful to New Writing North, Creative Scotland and The Society of Authors for financial assistance – and encouragement – at crucial stages.

Sam Buchan-Watts is the author of *Faber New Poets 15* and co-editor, with Lavinia Singer, of *Try To Be Better* (Prototype), a creative-critical engagement with W. S. Graham. He is the recipient of an Eric Gregory Award (2016) and a Northern Writers' Award for Poetry (2019). In 2018 he undertook a fellowship at the Yale Center for British Art and he is currently a Leverhulme Early Career Fellow at Newcastle University.

### ABOUT PROTOTYPE

*Creating new possibilities in the publishing of fiction and poetry through a flexible, interdisciplinary approach and the production of unique and beautiful books.*

Prototype is an independent publisher working across genres and disciplines, committed to discovering and sharing work that exists outside the mainstream. Each publication is unique in its form and presentation, and the aesthetic of each object is considered critical to its production.

Prototype strives to increase audiences for experimental writing, as the home for writers and artists whose work requires a creative vision not offered by mainstream literary publishers. In its current, evolving form, Prototype consists of 4 strands of publications:

(type 1 — poetry)
(type 2 — prose)
(type 3 — interdisciplinary projects)
(type 4 — anthologies) including an annual anthology
of new work, *PROTOTYPE*.

*Path Through Wood* by Sam Buchan-Watts
Published by Prototype in 2021

Design by Matthew Stuart & Andrew Walsh-Lister (or Traven T. Croves)
Typeset in DTL Elzevir by Gerard Daniëls
Printed in Lithuania by KOPA

Cover image: detail from John Constable's *Cloud Study, Hampstead, Tree
at Right* (1821), reproduced with the kind permission of the Royal Academy
of Art, London; photo credit: © Royal Academy of Arts, London;
photographer: John Hammond

ISBN 978-1-913513-11-5


(          )  ( )    prototype     p

(type 1 – poetry)
www.prototypepublishing.co.uk
@prototypepubs

prototype publishing
71 oriel road
london e9 5sg
uk

*This is a book poised between delicacy and ferocity, itinerary and distillation: like the cloud forms and studies evoked here, these poems are shifting, mutable, provocatively shimmering condensations.* Path Through Wood *channels a paradoxically controlled dreamstate alert as well to the shit and pith of life – 'the skatepark put/naturally with the cesspit'. Welcome to our common permeability, vulnerability; welcome to the Anthropocene (or is it the Capitalocene? – terms this poet of immanent apprehensions need not use): 'I dreamt the pigeons were stressful to look at because of their own stress'. These poems are consistently surprising; they are also ethically alert to the question of 'staking common ground'. Refugees, prisons, questions of asylum; intimacies and boundaries; boyhood, masculinity, what it is to be 'one with others' (viz. C.D. Wright): all here, in ways rich, strange, sensuous, sonically gorgeous. Buchan-Watts' work infiltrates: vibrations, colours, signage pulse in the mind and along the skin. We tune in here to a kind of 'condensation after the internet'. This is work of but not bound to our dystopic networked surveilled condition; the poems have the unusual quality of being both highly wrought and freely aerated. The poet's deep, attentive, and skewed listening tracks a sensorium enmeshed and enmired and occasionally enchanted; his work is unparaphrasable yet feels inevitable. Henry Darger, John Ashbery, Vladimir Nabokov, Denise Riley are some of the tutelary spirits of a work both visionary and vernacular. A sounding, a probing, a measuring, a listening in, a 'colouring in' (as one bravura piece is titled): these are some of the many ways Buchan-Watts moves on this path through wood.*
    Maureen N. McLane

*The poet Robert Frost once said 'I don't like obscurity or obfuscation, but I do like dark sayings I must leave the clearing of to time'. Buchan-Watts takes a path less travelled through language and listening in this artful and compelling debut of labyrinthine repetition and reverberation, inviting the reader on a circular journey to find their own clearings.*
    Rachael Boast

*Contemplation and violence, and the purpose of art, are among the complex themes in this formally inventive and persistently alert, allusive collection that had me enthralled. I've been following Sam's work since the astonishing pamphlet with Faber & Faber, and this debut is just as impressive!*
    Daljit Nagra

*This is poetry of stylish incisiveness and fascinating intelligence. Buchan-Watts has digested a wide range of disparate and incongruous influences and inspirations only to speak in his own unusually distinctive voice. The tempered exuberance of these poems – their new kind of storytelling, their strangely evocative coherence – is at once alluring and disarming. It is a very remarkable book.*
  Adam Phillips

*In this accumulating revelation of a book, Sam Buchan-Watts makes visible music from the kinds of vernacular incantations that define our restless path through the dark wood at the center of human life. Like innovators in verse before him, he unfolds a sonic vista to reveal the expanding vernacular as the deep landscape of promise and danger it is. It's been said if you see deeply enough you will see musically. Attuned perhaps preternaturally to such a music, Buchan-Watts demonstrates in his empathetic poems how the individuals who repeat the common refrains, though in doing so they are not unique, may yet be profound. Poetry will feel the impact of* Path Through Wood *for many years.*
  Douglas Crase

*One of the most playful and cerebral poets of our time, Sam Buchan-Watts in his debut* Path Through Wood *generates a nervous energy that reflects our age of anxiety about the interconnectedness between existence and extinction, liberty and injustice, sense and nonsense, sound and sight, clouds and trees. His poems evaporate and condense like dreamworks that reveal the intimacy and puzzlement of listening, colouring, remembering and desiring. Fearlessly inventive and microscopically curious, he observes the physical and metaphysical worlds through 'the threshold between inner and outer ear', with wit, style and candour that remind us of Constable, W.S. Graham, and Denise Riley.*
  Kit Fan

*These are poems which are capable of announcing themselves in pleasingly familiar and vernacular terms, whilst almost simultaneously being able to engage with a more concise and rapid and high-lyric voice. We were blown away by how Buchan-Watts was able to fuse academic thinking with emotion in these taut and musical poems, balancing 'well-weighed syllables' with 'WhatsApp messages' to find his own unique voice.*
  Richard Scott, Ivan Juritz Prize judge

*tincture of the skies*